The Opening of the Cherokee Outlet, Oklahoma

Anthony F. Rice

General Land Office

1893

Note: The Cherokee Outlet was opened to settlement at noon, Central Standard Time, September 16, 1893. The opening was participated in by more than 115,000 persons. The work was supervised on the ground by 45 employees of the General Land Office. The Outlet, excluding reservations, contained nearly 6,500,000 acres, an area sufficient to make about 40,000 homestead claims of 160.acres each. Anthony F. Rice was an employee of the General Land Office in 1893, who assisted in the opening of these lands. This paper chronicles what he saw during this time in Oklahoma history.

To step from Perry, O.T., as it was when I was there in 1893, into this handsome library, is like taking a sudden jump from Sheol into Heaven.

Before reading this paper, I wish to state that if any one expects a high-grade literary dissertation on this subject, he will be disappointed. There was nothing of a literary nature connected with this matter. It was a "Public Land Opening," in its wildest country, and wildest sense. A public land opening is one of the first marks of the march of progress and civilization. This opening is the history of all public land openings and differs from the others only in that on account of its magnitude, it was a little more pronounced.

I will attempt to describe it as I saw it and as it in reality was.

In 1808 the Cherokee Indians, who lived in North Caroline, Georgia and Tennessee, sent here to Washington two deputations of said Indians, known as the Upper Cherokee Towns and Lower Cherokee Towns. They called upon the President and made the following representations:

The Upper Towns contingent said that the Cherokees whom they represented wished to engage in the pursuits of agriculture and civilized life, and therefore wished to remain undisturbed. The delegation of the Lower Towns stated that their followers desired to continue to live as hunters, and therefore, owing to the scarcity of game in their present neighborhood, they wanted to move west of the Mississippi River.

In 1809 the President replied that the wishes of both factions would be granted. An Indian exploring party was organized and sent out in search of a place suitable to their taste. The party returned and reported as their choice a section of the country lying on the Arkansas and White Rivers.

In 1817 a treaty was made, under which the Cherokees received as much land of the place selected as they gave up east of the Mississippi River.

This treaty, together with subsequent treaties entered into by the Cherokees and the Muscogee or Creek Indians of Alabama and Georgia, and the Choctaw Indians of

Mississippi and Alabama, resulted in the removal of the Indians to what is now known as the Indian Territory.

All of Oklahoma Territory was carved out of this Territory except "No Man's Land." The first portion of the Territory was opened up in April, 1889.

The Cherokees became possessed of the "Strip" or "Perpetual Outlet West," under the treaty of May 6, 1868. It is about 225 miles long and 58 miles wide, and contains in round numbers, 8,145,000 acres.

"No Man's Land" is about 167 miles

long and 34 ½ miles wide, and contains 3,681,000 acres. This was acquired by the United States from Texas in 1850. When it was proposed in the 33rd Congress, to establish the Territory of Nebraska, it was discovered. that the southern boundary thereof, which was fixed in the bill at 36 degrees and 30 minutes north latitude, would divide the Cherokee Nation. In order to avoid this, the line, which finally became the southern boundary of the Territory of Kansas, was drawn at 37 degrees north latitude. That still left this Strip of land unattached to any State or Territory, or any judicial district. Hence the name "No Man's Land."

Its inhabitants, numbering about 15,000 in 1889, had some schools and churches and were under no protection and under no restraint whatever. They were as free as the birds in the air. If you did not like your neighbor, you could "do him up," providing always you "got the drop on him." Many conflicts took place between the settlers and cattlemen, in which the settlers usually came out "second best."

The people of Oklahoma were all in the

same box, for more than a year, as the people of "No Man's Land." The Territory was organized in May (2) 1890, and took in what was heretofore known and referred to as "No Man's Land."

The portion known as the "Outlet" was purchased from the Cherokees and other Indians, who were in possession, in pursuance of the Acts of 1885 and 1889. A part of this Outlet, embracing about 6,500,000 acres, was opened up in September, 1893.

Now we will come to the question of who had a right to enter this land. I will be as brief as possible. Any citizen of the United States, or any person who has declared his intention to become such, and who is 21 years of age, or the head of a family, and who had not previously exhausted his right, and is not the owner of 160 acres of land, is qualified to initiate a homestead entry. After residing on the land for at least 5 years and cultivating the same for that period, the parties will, upon furnishing the required proof thereof, and paying the price set by the Government, which ranges from $1.00 to $2.50 per acre, eventually receive a patent from the

Government.

When parties had satisfactorily established their right to enter for either a homestead or town lot, they were given certificates allowing them to run in at the appointed time of opening.

The Government established seven townsites, each containing 320 acres, named Perry, Pawnee, Alva, Enid and Round Pound, Newkirk, and Woodward, four of which had a land office. These townsite lands were surveyed and platted into blocks, lots, streets and alleys. Parties desiring to secure lots were required to show their qualifications at the booths, which was merely to the effect that they were native-born or naturalized citizens of the United States, or had declared their intention to become such.

The Board of Trustees approved by the Secretary of the Interior value each lot and assess upon the whole number of lots, a sum sufficient to pay for the land embraced in the town, which amount runs from $320 to $800, according to its location in the Territory, and an additional sum to cover the cost of entry, survey, execution of deeds, etc.

In order to obtain a deed, the party must appear before the Board of Trustees and show that he went upon and occupied the lot prior to any other person. Upon doing this satisfactorily he receives his deed.

In case two or more parties claim the same lot, the Boards order a hearing to determine their respective rights. In order to insure the costs, each party is required to deposit a day's cost of the hearing, on each morning. Each party is allowed to introduce evidence. The party dissatisfied with the decision can appeal, in thirty days, to the

Commissioner of the General Land Office, and from him, in sixty days, to the Secretary of the Interior. No costs accrue after the case leaves the Board.

If the case is decided against all the parties in interest, the lot is sold for the benefit of the town or deeded to the town for public use, as the Secretary of the Interior may in his discretion direct.

Another way of establishing a town is as follows: If a party made a homestead entry and the land is afterwards required for townsite purposes, he may commute his entry at $10 per acre (less the cost of from 10 to 20 acres, which he must donate for public uses), after showing that he had com- plied with the homestead laws up to date of this application and that the land is required for townsite purposes, and must accompany his application by a plat. He then gets a patent for the land and disposes of the lots at such a price as he sees fit.

The money which he paid to the United States for the land is paid into the town treasury by the United States after the town has been organized into a municipality.

If two parties claim the same piece of land under the homestead law, the hearing is ordered by the local land officers and the appeal lies the same as in town-lot cases.In case both parties prove simultaneous settlement the land goes to the higher bidder of the two.

In order to prevent parties who had no rights under the homestead laws from entering upon the land and thereby defeat the chance of those who were entitled thereto, the "booth" or registration system was adopted. Accordingly, nine booths were established, five of which were on the northern and four on the southern line of the Outlet.

Forty-five clerks were detailed for duty at the booths. We assembled at Wichita, Kansas, before proceeding to our respective points of destination. The party in which I was went to Kiowa., Kansas. This town is a border-town, containing about 700 people. We stopped at the best hotel in town. It was a $2.00 a day concern and was blown full of bullet holes.

The meats served were like rubber, while the biscuits were more available as fishing sinkers than anything else. The proprietor's brother said things were "high now, eggs costing 8 3/4¢ a dozen. I was paying S2.00 for four together with a little iced tea.

When one of the clerks asked to have his baggage checked to Goodwin, Texas, the baggage master exclaimed, "My God, Man, This is the first piece of baggage ever sent to that place and will be the last." The clerk describes Goodwin as nothing but "a board nailed up." He did not stop there but went to Higgins. Higgins is a big Texas town, containing 10 or 12 houses, one of which is occupied by a bank, doing a large business. (Perhaps it's a faro-bank).

The booths were open from September 11, to September 19, 1893, between the hours of 7 A.M. and 6 P.M. Over 115,000 persons registered, while the lands fit for homesteading would provide for only about 20,000. Of course many went in for town lots. More than half of the land is suitable for grazing only.

I registered a blind man and in order to satisfy my curiosity, I inquired of his guardian what possible chance the poor fellow had in this wild scramble and how he proposed to make the race. The guardian replied that he would stand him on the line and as soon as the gun was fired, he would make one jump and plant his flag. I am afraid that this fellow, if he got in front of that crowd, was himself planted, instead of the flag.

The hardships endured were indescribable. Persons slept on the line for two or three days, waiting to be registered. Hot winds were blowing the sand-dust was carried in clouds and the heat of the sun was terrific; but no sunstrokes so far as I know.

The nights were almost cold. Water was scarce. Thank heaven, some other liquids were not quite so scarce though rather high priced. When we arrived in the morning at the booths, those who slept on the line, for fear of losing their places, without as much as a blanket or shawl to cover themselves, were stiff with cold and thawed out later in the day by the rays of the sun which they then so gladly welcomed.

While the registration system caused considerable hardship of a temporary nature, it was more than balanced by far, in the vast amount of permanent good accomplished by way of preventing fraud. Many a man no doubt owes his house and farm to this system.

And all this was endured for what? In the bare hope of realizing that which is so characteristic of our present speculative generation -- the desire to get "something for nothing."

At the booth near Arkansas City, several ladies asked to be allowed to register without being compelled to continue to stand in line, which was working a hardship on them. As the officers in charge had no authority to grant this privilege, a red-headed Kentucky Colonel made a speech to the throng of men in which he earnestly plead for the ladies. The men consented.

In a few moments 986 were in line. The eyes of the men began to bulge, some groaned, but on the whole they faced the racket quite well.

At high noon on September 16, 1893, the soldiers fired their guns, and off started the greatest and most wonderful race of all times. About 150,000 persons went pell mall-helter skelter. They were old and young, of both sexes, the strong, the sick, the crippled, deaf, dumb and blind. Some went in on horseback, some in vehicles of every conceivable description, and of no description, some by train and some on foot.

The trains were loaded. Every inch of the roofs were covered and many hung on the sides of the cars by holding to the window sills, while the open windows furnished room for some.

Talk about hurdle and cross country races? You should have witnessed this one. It was a beautiful sight. I'll not forget it for many a day. First one man dismounted and planted his flag, in an instant another, then perhaps a woman, and then in a moment more they dismounted by the hundred. They dropped so quick one would imagine they dropped from the clouds, like rain ·drops, while some seemed to come up from under the turf. They were here, there and everywhere. Now and then you would hear the words: "There's a sooner, shoot him, shoot him, shoot the....----he's a sooner." Bang. ---- (A sooner is a person who went on the land too soon. That is, before the hour of opening.)

It was a race in which according to racing parlance, no man bad a "double lead pipe cinch." It was a race in which everybody was out in dead earnest, for the "dust." (And by the way that is about all most of them got).

All sorts of tricks were resorted to, to get ahead of others.

One man, seeing a woman behind him on the same piece of land, left it and ran for another piece in order to give her a show. After he was out of sight, she pulled off her wrapper and behold? There stood a man, in full and undisputed possession of a nice tract of land.

At noon, not a house or tent was there except the land and post offices, and a few small railroad houses, In a few hours thereafter, large towns were in full working order, under tents and making preparations to annex the suburbs. Washington's real estate boomers are not in it with the lads down there. Stages were run to the inland towns. It was a scene of activity. Everything was humming.

That night I slept on the bare floor of the

land office at Alva. The next night, Sunday, I slept in the second story of a. bunk erected in the cellar of a railroad house.

Services were held in the open air Sunday morning and in the evening by the aid of candles. The preacher who held services in the evening, took as his text, "A good tree bringeth forth good fruit." After holding strictly to the intention of the text for a few minutes, he spent nearly an hour in endeavoring to encourse the planting of good trees. I learned afterwards that he was engaged in the nursery business in Southern Kansas.

And such an incongruous conglomerated aggregation of people that made up the city of Perry (there were about 20,000 there), you should have seen. All nationalities, and all of us one color - the color of the sand that stuck to us and which no one escaped. The "has beens" and "wood be's" of politics, the plain farmer, the boomer, a number of gentlemen, the rough and ready, the riff-raff, the outlaws and outcasts of society in general, were all there. The streets, alleys, parks, and government reservations were all covered with tents, shacks, sod-houses, dug-outs, etc. Many a poor fellow thought he was holding down a $1000 lot, only to find out in the course of a few days that he was sitting in the street or alley.

One section of the city became known as "Hell's half acre." And indeed, it's the only name that begins to tell the kind of a place it was. The guy ropes of one tent crossed those of the other. You would jump over one only to be caught by another. It seemed to have an innumerable number of gambling houses and such other houses as always thrive in a neighborhood of that character. Dance houses were there and prize fighting galore. It defies description. It would have been a fit place for exhibit at and would have capped the climax in the Midway Plaisance. The first hotel was located there and was known as the "Wild West." It had no walls, or roof, except the boundless sky. The best sleep I had during my stay of six weeks in the Territory was there. The beds were all new and about six inches apart. I slept with all of my clothes on, even my hat. The shoes which I had under the bed,

I pulled in for fear they would fit some other fellow before morning. When I awoke, I was covered with sand and found a woman on the right side of me - in the adjoining bed - covered up to the top of her forehead.

The only decent wash I had while there, was when we received a barrel of waukesha water. It was spoiled for drinking purposes, when it arrived. So we borrowed a tub and one fellow stood in it while the other kindly scrubbed him. The water rolled down as dirty as in the streets of Alexandria during a rain. The sand blew right into us, I inferred from the old axiom "Every man must eat a peck of dirt," that after he did so, his time to die had come. This is not true, gentlemen. I'm a living witness. Hundreds of us ate bushels of it.

In order to see what was contained in the standing dishes in the so- called eating houses, it was frequently necessary to take a knife and first scrape off some of good Mother Earth its surface. The water was mostly salty or full of alkali. No deep wells

Perry was a place where the policy of "Everybody for himself and God for us all," was carried out to its logical conclusion.

About 18 were killed while I was there among whom was "Three Fingered Jack" or "Texas Jack," a member of the saintly Bill Dalton gang of outlaws. I carried a $5.00 note, as a souvenier, for a long time, which was covered with the blood that oozed from his wounds.

This· place was also "No Man's Land" for over 30 days. Men were murdered and no questions asked. Pistol shots were fired through tents in which people stood or slept, just for fun.

(Describe the taking off of Stevens). About his partner's story of the affair. He died with a smile of contempt - a cast iron smile of unsatisfied revenge upon his countenance. I'll see it as long as I live. This was an ideal community, Gentlemen, for men who do not believe in having constituted authorities.

There were from 300 to 400 lawyers there, mostly jack legs, sharpers, shysters, smooth gentlemen, and unprincipled scoundrels, two banks, 28 lumber yards, and over 60 grocery stores, several daily papers,· a circus, dime museums, and so on and so on.

Before the opening some men were asking "which town are the women going to." I couldn't understand why they wanted to know that. Later on I heard many frontiersmen remark that "where the gamblers and dissolute women go, there stands a good town." Accepting this as the standard of measurement, Perry was a "Lulu."

Its sanitary condition needs no comment, and defies it.

The newly elected Mayor was quoted as having said in an interview, that the policy of the city is to be "a wide open one." That is, gambling houses will be permitted to flourish upon payment of a fine of so much per table and disreputable women will not be disturbed so long as they pay their fines regularly. But there must be respect of law everywhere. (Hum.)

I have no doubt that the better element of the bad element soon got in control. The people are now perhaps governed by an element whose standing would average as well as they do in most places today.

You have often heard tell of doing a "Land Office Business." We did it there.

About 12,000 persons were in line, suspicious and all clamoring for admission at once.

Excitement ran high and was at fever heat. Dead beats were willing to pay to have a chance to cheat or bleed someone, while honest men were willing to bribe in order to ·escape the sharks. Owing to the dirt storms, the doors were barred and the applications received through a small opening made by the raising of a window. But is just didn't seem to do much good. The dust blew ·right through the boards. If we wanted to blow the dust off the papers before writing, we would still be blowing. A large pistol was lying on the table desk, between the Register of the Land Office and myself, ready for service. About 10 deputy U.S. Marshalls were doing duty at the door and window, "armed to their teeth." (Describes how they were armed).

One man in an advanced stage of typhoid fever was carried to the window on a stretcher in order to file. The crowd permitted him to go to the head of the line. Men who lost their places in line brought all sorts of affidavits in an endeavor to get back again. Some of them were very loosely drawn. I'll give you two of them. One man furnished an affidavit giving the reason for having lost his place in line, because his daughter had the "material" fever. (Meant malarial). The other read because his wife was "prostituted" on the prairie. (Meant prostrated.)

Scenes took place that would melt a heart of granite. One morning, a woman with a baby on her arms, not yet three weeks old, came to the office to be allowed to go ahead of the line in order to file her claim. She reported that her husband had been choked to death on his claim. The murdered man was big and strong. It probably took four men   to "get away with him." The skin on the back of his hands and elbows was rubbed off to the very bones, by his frantic efforts to release himself. He was not robbed. The motive, evidently, was to get the land.

The poor widow, already made weak by her confinement and the shock of her husband's death, was still further set back by being informed that several applications were already filed for this particular piece of land. This meant that she could institute an expensive contest, the result of which is at best   uncertain. No less than eight

applications are now pending for the tract.

According to the Governor's report for

1894, Oklahoma had a population of 212,000

which netted a church membership estimated

at 15,000, of whom over 9,000 are Catholics.

School population is 74,384. It has one

University, at Norman, with 147 students; one

Normal School at Edmond, with 116 students;

one agricultural and Mechanical college, at

Stillwater, with 100 students. No   charge   is

made or tuition. A student can go through the

college year at an expense of about $160, exclusive of clothing.

The schools and colleges were all aided by the Federal Government. She had about 1,250,000 acres granted for that purpose, which yield (from its leases) a revenue of about $100,000 a year.

Oklahoma at the "Fair."

The eastern section is very fertile. She received first prize for wheat and second for flour. The Governor says that the flour which received first prize was made from Oklahoma wheat. She also received awards for corn, oats, buckwheat, grass, peanuts, red sorghum, squashes, cotton, and - guess what? Painted China, which was the work of a Guthrie woman.

Among other things which thrive there, are grapes, watermelons, sweet and Irish potatoes. Also centipedes and tarantulas.

27548503R00028

Made in the USA
Lexington, KY
13 November 2013